Dr. Gregory Boya's
MYTH OF A CHRISTIAN NATION:
A Reply, Refutation and Rebuttal

DR. GREGORY BOYD'S
MYTH OF A CHRISTIAN NATION

A REPLY, REFUTATION AND REBUTTAL

BY
JOHN TELLER

Dr. Gregory Boyd's
MYTH OF A CHRISTIAN NATION:
A Reply, Refutation and Rebuttal

ISBN (13) (Paperback): 978-1-68109-015-3
ISBN (10) (Paperback): 1-68109-015-5
ISBN (13) (Kindle): 978-1-68109-016-0
ISBN (10) (Kindle): 1-68109-016-3
ISBN (13) (ePub): 978-1-68109-017-7
ISBN (10) (ePub): 1-68109-017-1

Time Books™
an imprint of TellerBooks™
TellerBooks.com/Time_Books

www.TellerBooks.com

Manufactured in the U.S.A.

NOTE: Unless otherwise stated herein, all biblical Scriptures quoted herein are taken from the New King James Version or American Standard Version translations, unless the verses are quoted directly from Dr. Gregory Boyd's book, in which case other translations may be used.

DISCLAIMER: The opinions, views, positions and conclusions expressed in this volume reflect those of the individual author and not necessarily those of the publisher or any of its imprints, editors or employees.

ABOUT THE IMPRINT

The *Reply, Refutation and Rebuttal* Series™ of Time Books™ publishes monographs and treatises that reply to contemporary perspectives on political, philosophical and religious issues.

Complete your collection with the following titles:

- Dinesh D'Souza's *What's So Great About America*: A Reply, Refutation and Rebuttal
- Dr. Gregory Boyd's *Myth of a Christian Nation:* A Reply, Refutation and Rebuttal
- Dr. Mel White's *What the Bible Says and Doesn't Say About Homosexuality*: A Reply, Refutation and Rebuttal
- Dr. H. M. Baagil's *Muslim-Christian Dialogue*: A Reply, Refutation and Rebuttal
- *The Communist Manifesto* of Karl Marx and Friedrich Engels: A Reply, Refutation and Rebuttal

The mission of Time Books™ is to reintroduce time-tested values and truths to modern debates on political, economic, and moral issues. The imprint focuses on books and monographs dealing with society, ethics, and public policy.

CONTENTS

ABBREVIATIONS

English Translations of the Bible:

ASV...............American Standard Version
BBE...............Bible in Basic English
Darby.............Darby Bible
ESV ....English Standard Version
ISV ....International Standard Version
KJV ....King James Version
MKJV............Modern King James Version
NIV ....New International Version
NKJV ....New King James Version
RSV...............Revised Standard Version

Books of the Bible:
1Ch...............1 Chronicles
1Co................1 Corinthians
1Jn.................1 John
1Ki.................1 Kings
1Pe.................1 Peter
1Sa.................1 Samuel
1Th ....1 Thessalonians
1Ti..................1 Timothy
2Ch.................2 Chronicles
2Co.................2 Corinthians
2Jn..................2 John
2Ki.................2 Kings
2Pe.................2 Peter
2Sa.................2 Samuel
2Th ....2 Thessalonians
2Ti..................2 Timothy
3Jo ....3 John
Acts ....Book of Acts
Amos ....Book of Amos
Col..................Colossians

Dan................Daniel
Deu................Deuteronomy
Ecc.................Ecclesiastes
Eph.................Ephesians
Est ....Esther
Exo ....Exodus
Eze.................Ezekiel
Ezr.................Book of Ezra
Gal.................Galatians
Gen.................Genesis
Hab.................Habakkuk
Hag.................Haggai
Heb.................Hebrews
Hos.................Hosea
Isa...................Isaiah
Jas..................James
Jer..................Jeremiah
Job..................Book of Job
Joel ....Book of Joel
John.................Gospel of John
Jon..................Jonah
Jos ....Joshua
Jude ....Book of Jude
Jdg..................Judges
Lam ....Lamentations
Lev ....Leviticus
Luke ....Gospel of Luke
Mal ....Malachi
Mark...............Gospel of Mark
Mat ....Gospel of Matthew
Mic ....Micah
Nah.................Nahum
Neh.................Nehemiah
Num.................Numbers
Oba.................Obadiah
Phm ....Philemon
Php ....Philippians
Pro ....Proverbs

Psa...................Psalms
Rev.................Revelation
Rom................Romans
Ruth................Book of Ruth
Son ....Song of Solomon
Tit....................Titus
Zec..................Zechariah
Zep ....Zephaniah

CHAPTER 1. INTRODUCTION

In his best-selling book, *The Myth of a Christian Nation,* Dr. Gregory Boyd, a widely-respected theologian and pastor, argues that the church was established to serve the world with a Christ-like love that is diametrically opposed to the pursuit of political power. Christians are called to manifest a "kingdom of the cross" that impacts culture through self-sacrificial love, not the Romans 13 "kingdom of the sword" that impacts culture through coercive force.

Dr. Boyd's radical separatism leaves committed Christians with no choice other than to abandon the civic realm. His is a call to effect change through spiritual disciplines, such as prayer, not by taking up the reins of government to exercise "power over" others. For Boyd, there is no room for Christians to serve in government or any of its arms, including the military or police.

At last—there is now a reply, refutation and rebuttal to Dr. Boyd's treatise and conclusions, which result from misunderstandings of fundamental biblical principles and the selective treatment of Scripture. This volume, , the latest in Time Books' *Reply, Refutation and Rebuttal Series™,* systematically replies to each of Dr. Boyd's arguments against Christians' participation in civil government, the military and other civil institutions. This rebuttal to Dr. Boyd's treatise shows that far from being called to eschew the "power over" kingdom of the sword, Christians are called to be God's co-laborers in redeeming the kingdom of sword, just as they are called to transform every other aspect of the fallen creation.

The overall goal of this volume is to leave the reader with an understanding of God's sovereignty and lordship over all of creation, as taught in the Scripture, and to call man to partner with God in restoring the brokenness of creation, eschewing Dr. Boyd's radical separatism.

CHAPTER 2. CHRISTIAN PACIFISM AND NON-VIOLENCE

I. OUR LIFE PURPOSE IS TO LOVE, SERVE AND LOOK AFTER THE INTERESTS OF OTHERS

A. Dr. Boyd's Argument

Dr. Gregory Boyd begins by laying out as the central purpose of the Christian life doing all things in love. We must "do 'nothing from selfish ambition or conceit, but in humility regard others as better than [our]selves.' We are to 'look not to [our] own interests, but to the interest of others" (Phil. 2:3-4) ... Following Jesus' example, we are to find honor in washing people's feet ..., in serving them in any way we can" (p. 31). Living in Calvary-like love "moment by moment, in all circumstances and in relation to all people, is the sole calling of those who are aligned with the kingdom that Jesus came to bring" (p. 32).

Any form of religion void of radical love is empty and useless. "[I]f we don't look like Jesus Christ carrying his cross to Golgotha—sacrificing our time, energy, and resources for others—our rightness is merely religious noise ... However right we may be, without love we are simply displaying a religious version of the world, not the kingdom of God" (p. 49).

B. Rebuttal: War as Charity

The social thinker George Weigel notes that since St. Augustine, just-war thinking has been based on the "classic moral judgment" that legitimate public authorities have the moral obligation "to pursue justice ... even at risk to themselves and those for whom they are responsible" (George Weigel, "The Catholic Difference: Getting 'Just War' Straight"). Therefore, a just war can be an act of charity in pursuit of justice (see Fr. Richard John Neuhaus, "Just War Is an Obligation of Charity," *National Catholic Register*, October 7-13, 2001, p. 8).

Some will point to God's commands to utterly destroy entire peoples, such as the Amorites and the Canaanites (Deu 7:1) cannot be an act of love or charity and therefore contradicts Christ's injunction to love one's neighbor. But it is precisely because the Bible cannot contradict itself that we are to understand the violence commanded by God as compatible with Christ's love. This violence may perhaps be understood as a means to prevent these peoples from breaking the most important commandment, forbidding the worship of other gods before God (Exo 20:30). This is why God later commands the Israelites to "destroy their altars, break down their sacred pillars and cut down their wooden images, and burn their carved images with fire" (Deu 7:5). The punishment may also implemented to highlight the vastness of God's mercy, for it is only when the starkness of God's justice is illustrated that one comes to appreciate His mercy: though we are all deserving of the death that the Amorites and Canaanites suffered, we are given new life and forgiveness through Christ.

Given Christ's command to love one's neighbor *and one's enemy*, we can only conclude that the violence and war commanded of God in the Old Testament was meant to be carried out in a spirit of love—love for God, love for justice and love of neighbor. Just as a loving Christian should report a child-abusing neighbor to the police out of a love for justice, so too should he do it out of love for the neighbor, a love of seeing the neighbor reformed. The intervention of the civil authorities may bring an end to the neighbor's iniquity, either through detention or otherwise through deterrence. Such an intervention, whether it results in prosecution and imprisonment or even acquittal, may lead to the end of behavior which might otherwise continue or spiral out of control.

We must always remember that even the Old Testament commanded the love of enemies (consider Proverbs: If your enemy is in need of food, give him bread; if he is in need of drink, give him water. For so you will put coals of fire on his head, and the Lord will give you your reward (Pro 25:21-22). Therefore, if we are to accept that all of the Scripture is God-breathed (2Ti 3:16), we must read the commandments to destroy Israel's enemies as given in a spirit of love.

Some may argue that it was said in the Old Testament to hate one's enemies, since Jesus preached, "You have heard it said, You shall love your neighbor and hate your enemy (Mat 5:43). However, "hate your enemy" was never commanded by any of the prophets. Fr. Cornelius a Lapide explains this by writing that "this saying was not in the Law, but was said by the Scribes who interpreted the Law. For they, because they found in Lev. xix. 18, 'Thou shalt love thy neighbour,' or 'thy friend,' as the Vulgate translates, inferred from thence that they should hate their enemies. Wherefore Christ here corrects this interpretation of theirs, and explains the Law, that by neighbor or friend every man is meant, even a foreigner, a Gentile, and an enemy. For all men are neighbors, through their first forefather, Adam, and brethren one of another. We are also brethren through our second Father, Christ, through whom we have been born again, and, as it were, created anew in the likeness of God, and called to the common inheritance of God, our Father in heaven." Hence, Christ abolishes the false teachings and legal misinterpretations of the Scribes and restores the original meaning of the Scriptures.

One thus finds that love permeates the Old Testament law. The wars commanded of the Israelites can only be understood within this context, and must thus have been waged in accordance with the commandment of love.

For further discussion on how love for neighbor can warrant the just use of force, see J. Daryl Charles, *Between Pacifism and Jihad: Just War and Christian Tradition*, which discusses the Church's just-war teaching on the use of force to maintain or reestablish justice and answers many of the concerns of the pacifist position while deliberately avoiding the excesses of militarism.

II. THE KINGDOM OF GOD DOES NOT ADVANCE BY VIOLENCE; WE SHOULD EFFECT CHANGE THROUGH NONVIOLENCE

Boyd further bolsters his take on non-violence by discussing Jesus' reprimand to the misguided disciple who struck the ear off one of the solders that came to arrest him. Boyd writes (p. 28):

One of his misguided disciples even tried to fight like a kingdom-of-the-world participant, cutting off the ear of one of the soldiers who came to arrest Jesus. Jesus rebuked the disciple and demonstrated the nature of his unique heavenly kingdom by healing the soldier's ear (Luke 22:50-51), showing that his kingdom would advance not by destroying the enemy who seeks to destroy you, but by loving, serving, and hopefully transforming the enemy who seeks to destroy you.

Boyd lays out a division between the two kingdoms that Christians will find themselves immersed in: The kingdom of God to which Jesus calls us and the kingdom of the world, comprised of civil governments. As citizens of kingdoms of the world, Christians should always eschew violence and trust holy living and prayer over the power of the sword. He writes (p. 41):

Martin Luther King Jr. captured the heart of Jesus' ethic of loving one's enemy as he discussed the concept of nonviolent resistance advocated by Mahatma Gandhi (who himself was influenced by Christ's teachings). King wrote that the concept of *Satyagraha* (meaning 'power of love and truth') "avoids not only external physical violence but also violence of spirit. The nonviolent resister not only refuses to shoot his opponent but he also refuses to hate him.' Later, King commented, 'Along the way of life, someone must have sense enough and morality enough to cut off the chain of hate. This can be done by projecting the ethic of love to the center of our lives ... When put into practice ..., loving one's enemies and returning evil with good has a power to accomplish something the kingdom of the sword can never dream of: namely, freeing the enemy from his hatred and stopping the ceaseless cycle of violence that hatred fuels.

III. "DO NOT RESIST AN EVILDOER": VIOLENCE IS NOT JUSTIFIED EVEN IN SELF-DEFENSE

A. Boyd's Argument

Boyd quotes Jesus' teaching to not "resist an evildoer" (Mat 5:39) and St. Paul's teaching to never "repay anyone evil for evil" (Rom 12:17) and to "overcome evil with good" (Rom 12:21). It would seem from Jesus' command to not "resist an evildoer" and to "turn the other cheek" (Mat 5:39) (p. 162), that Christians are to passively allow evil to take place. Yet even Boyd recognizes that this is not the case: "[T]he word Jesus uses for 'resist' (*antistenai*) doesn't imply passively allowing something to take place. It rather connotes resisting a forceful action with a similar forceful action" (p. 163). Applying Jesus' command, then, a Christian who is assaulted should not assault his attacker. It does not, however, mean that the Christian should not complain to the authorities or have his attacker arrested. A Christian who is stolen from should not steal from his thief. He is not, however, to be impeded from filing a suit against the thief. Jesus is forbidding "responding to violent action with *similar* violent action. He's teaching us not to take on the violence of the one who is acting violently toward us. He's teaching us to respond to evil in a way that is consistent with loving them. But he's not by any means saying *do nothing*" (p. 163).

For the Christian, this can take many forms. It can mean, for example, setting up an alarm system around one's home rather than sleeping with a loaded gun to respond to a potential robber. It may mean reasoning with someone who treated him unfairly rather than hating or bearing a grudge against him.

As Boyd concedes, "Jesus' teachings "aren't a set of pacifistic laws people are to merely obey" (p. 164). Rather, they are "descriptions of what life in God's domain looks like and prescriptions for how we are to cultivate this alternative form of life" (p. 164). Thus, for Boyd, Jesus is trying to get us to a place where we are radically transformed, such that we naturally respond to our enemies in a loving way. Boyd explains that a person transformed by Jesus' love (p. 165):

> would *want* to do good to his attacker. This wouldn't be a matter of him trying to obey an irrational rule to "look for an alternative in extreme situations," for in extreme situations no one is thinking about obeying rules! Rather, it would be in the Christlike nature of this person to see nonviolent alternatives if they were present … Perhaps they'd see that pleading with, startling, or distracting the attacker would be enough to save themselves and their family.

Moreover, the person's "day-by-day surrender to God would have cultivated a sensitivity to God's Spirit that would enable him to discern God's leading in the moment" (p. 165). However, Boyd concedes that there will be situations in which a follower of Jesus will find no way to save himself or his family except through harming the attacker. Because Jesus would in this situation choose nonviolence, so should a true disciple of Jesus.

B. Rebuttal: "Do Not Resist an Evildoer": Jesus *Really* Means Do not Return Violence with the Same Kind of Violence

Boyd recognizes that by "do not resist an evildoer" (Mat 5:39), Jesus means do not return violence with the same kind of violence (*i.e.*, do not resist "a forceful action with a similar forceful action" (p. 163)). Boyd concludes that a Christian is to search for a non-violent alternative when responding to an evildoer. If the only alternative that exists is a violent one, a Christian should choose not exercise it. This might result in allowing an attacker to harm oneself or one's family. Boyd concedes the difficulty in reconciling how this could be moral (p. 167), but concludes that his job is to obey Chris, not rationalize His commandments.

Perhaps the difficulty that Boyd cites is the voice of reason tempering his interpretation of the Scripture and showing that it would *not* be moral to allow such harm. Would God not prefer a man to use non-deadly force to strike an attacker unconscious over allowing that attacker to harm or even murder the man's wife and children? Would it not be more in line with the model of the good Samaritan to knock the man down, call the police and the ambulance and then minister to the criminal while he is in the custody of the police or hospital, than to allow the man to harm or murder him and his family and then continue onward in his wicked ways?

Sometimes, the most loving approach to an evildoer is physical violence, for sometimes, if temporarily handicapping the physical members carrying out sin, one can then minister to the more important, eternal part of the man—his soul. God can always raise up and heal a broken bone or wounded limb, but an unrepenting soul does not find salvation (2Co 7:10).

And so just as a Christian is to seek every alternative to impede evildoers without doing them physical harm, in situations where physical harm is necessary, it should be undertaken with the least amount of harm (*e.g.*, striking an attacker on the head with the butt of a gun rather than shooting him). And this is how police forces and militaries and other civil authorities in nations influenced by Christianity should act—always looking to do the most good to evildoers by using the least amount of violence. Judges and prosecutors should seek to imprison criminals in order to deter them from further crime. Police should never use force unless necessary and then only non-deadly force (*e.g.*, using a baton or, when using a gun, shooting at a limb and not towards vital organs). Militaries should seek to wage war in a way that results in the least amount of harm to persons and property—taking down an enemy's radar stations, cratering runways and other targets that will incapacitate an enemy without causing loss of life or, where loss of life is necessary, protecting civilian populations and civilian objects such as hospitals, schools and places of religious worship. Yet in a nation that rejects Christian principles of love, none of these distinctions will have any place, nor will human life have any value as war is waged to produce the maximum amount of destruction to life and property.

IV. CHRISTIAN PARTICIPATION IN THE ROMANS 13 "SWORD" OF GOVERNMENT IS INCOMPATIBLE WITH THE ROMANS 12 INJUNCTION TO LOVE YOUR ENEMY

A. Boyd's Argument

As Boyd notes, "many have argued that they found grounds for a 'just war' exception to Jesus' teaching in Romans 13," which "grants that the authority of government ultimately comes from God and that God uses it to punish wrongdoers" (Rom 13:1-5) (p. 169). Yet Boyd argues that "while Paul encourages Christians to be *subject* to civil authority, he does not suggest that Christians should *participate* in the government's sword-wielding activity.

Rather, the Christian is to read Romans 13 in conjunction with Romans 12, which commands:

- *Bless those who persecute you*; do not curse them (Rom 12:14).
- *Do not repay evil for evil* (Rom 12:17).
- *Do not take avenge yourselves*, but give way to the wrath of God; for it is said, Punishment is mine, I will give reward, says the Lord (Rom 12:19).
- If *your enemy is hungry, feed him*; if *thirsty, give him drink*, for in so doing you will put coals of fire on his head (Rom 12:20).
- Do *not be overcome with evil*, but *overcome evil with good* (Rom 12:21).

In chapter 13, Paul specifies that sword-wielding authorities are one means by which God executes vengeance (13:4). Since this is the same vengeance disciples are *forbidden* to exercise (Rom 12:9), the "vengeance" that is recognized "as being within providential control when exercised by government is the same 'vengeance' that Christians are told not to exercise" (p. 169).

B. Rebuttal

Boyd establishes a red line in which Christians are not permitted to "exercise" Romans 13 vengeance and are therefore not to participate in the civil authority's sword-wielding. Presumably, this means that Christians are not to participate in militaries and police forces. What about as prosecutors? Presumably, since prosecutors execute judgment by seeking to punish criminals, they are exercising "vengeance" that for Boyd, is forbidden to Christians. What then about serving as judges? Judges at times find defendants guilty of crimes and sentence them to punishment. This vengeance is is forbidden to Christians. What about witnesses? A witness may testify that a defendant engaged in some wrong, thus leading to that defendant's conviction and punishment—also prohibited under Boyd's dichotomy. So if one follows Boyd's dichotomy to its full conclusion, a Christian who is assaulted, robbed, raped or is otherwise the victim of a violent crime should love and pray for his enemy but should in no way participate in the civil authority's vengeance for the crime. He or she should not report the crime to the police. She should not file a complaint or serve as a witness. She should not submit evidence to the courts or assist law enforcement in locating or arresting the defendant. Taken to its natural conclusion, Boyd's dichotomy essentially means that Christians are not to participate in retributive justice.

This view runs counter to God's divine appointment of civil authority to carry out his will. The purpose of civil government is to establish law, order and justice. It is to ensure retribution to criminals, ensure restitution to victims and deter evil. In a country influenced by Christianity, the government will achieve these ends. Christians who believe in the words of Abraham Kuyper that "there is not a square inch in the whole domain of our human existence over which Christ, who is Sovereign over all, does not cry: 'Mine!'" will recognize that it is their place to infiltrate every part of society—including the courts, the prisons, the police forces and the militaries—and ensure that God's will is done. In the case of civil government, God's will is clearly laid out in Romans 13. The conscientious Christian soldier, judge, lawyer or police officer is therefore to act in accordance with the commission to uphold justice, to ensure that civil institutions are never used for any other ends (to preserve the power of those in control, to steal from citizens, to oppress minorities, etc.) and to recognize that God is a God of justice and that His will is for justice on earth is to execute justice on wrongdoers.

The Christian's participation in the Romans 13 institutions of justice is in no way incompatible with the Romans 12 call to love one's enemies. Is it not more loving for a Christian to file a complaint against a criminal and see to his arrest and conviction and possibly even rehabilitation than to allow that criminal to continue in his ways? Is it not more in keeping with Christian character to cooperate with or even participate in the powers of the civil authority to see that a child molester, drug dealer or wife abuser is arrested and locked up than it is for him to refuse to participate in any way with the civil authority's justice? Is doing so not compatible with loving the criminal, praying for him and visiting him in jail and ministering to him? Is it perhaps not even preferable for the criminal's spiritual state for him to be stopped from his violent behavior and be put in a prison where he may have access to a chaplain or to Christians who may visit and minister to him, whereas if he continued in his sin he would never stop to question the path that his destructive ways were leading towards?

V. EVEN IF JUSTIFIED VIOLENCE IS AN EXCEPTION TO JESUS' TEACHING, POLITICAL FREEDOM IS NOT A JUST CAUSE FOR GOING TO WAR

A. Boyd's Argument

Boyd argues that even if justified violence is an exception to Jesus' teaching, political freedom is not a just cause for going to war (p. 170-71). He writes that we "kill and die for freedom and the freedom of others. But why should a kingdom person think killing for this reason is a legitimate exception to the New Testament's command to love and bless enemies? Can they be certain *God* holds this opinion" (p. 170). Boyd undermines the justification of many of America's military campaigns, undertaken under the pretext of "defending and spreading freedom" and argues that such a cause does not have any biblical support or precedent.

B. Rebuttal

In his second letter to the Corinthians, St. Paul writes that "where the Spirit of the Lord is, there is freedom" (2Co 3:17). Thus, wherever the spirit of God is, freedom prevails. Of course, the inverse is not true: just because there is freedom, the Spirit of God is not necessarily to be found. For example, Sodom and Gomorrah were marked by freedom in the sense that every man lived for himself and did what he pleased. But the Spirit of God did not inhabit these cities marked by sexual and violent freedom.

Nor does the Scripture raise up freedom to such a platform so as to justify killing. Boyd is correct in this respect. And there are other values that other cultures may hold that may equally compete with freedom. For example, in Muslim societies, it is virtue, not freedom, that is the supreme value of civil government and societal organization. Spreading "freedom" in Muslim lands would not serve as a just cause for war or invasion.

However, Christian just war theory has never held that spreading freedom constitutes a just cause that justifies armed conflict. The Catholic Church, which arguably has the most developed and precisely-elaborated just war theory of the Christian faith, clearly shows that the just cause required for armed conflict is self-defense (of the innocent) against an armed attack. In some views, redressing an injury, punishing evil or restoring territory unjustly seized are also deemed just causes. In any case, the central intention of the war must be re-establishing a just peace (not spreading freedom, conquering, spreading seeds of revolt or acquiring power or material possessions).

Therefore, "spreading freedom" would not constitute a just cause for the purpose of just war theory. However, this does not mean that there may not be wars with other causes in which the conscientious Christian may participate.

VI. EVEN IF SPREADING FREEDOM WERE A JUST CAUSE FOR WAR, OTHER FACTORS IMPEDE CHRISTIANS FROM MILITARY PARTICIPATION

A. Boyd's Argument

Next, Boyd argues that even if spreading freedom were a just cause for war, other factors, including the possibility that one's government is lying to him, impede the Christian from military participation. He writes (p. 171):

> Do you know—*can* you know—the myriad of personal, social, political, and historical factors that have led to any particular conflict to and bear upon whether or not it is 'justified'? For example, do you truly understand all the reasons your enemy gives for going to war against your nation, and are you certain they are altogether illegitimate? Are you certain your government has sought out all possible nonviolent means of resolving the conflict …? Are you certain the information you've been given about a war is complete, accurate, and objective? Do you know the *real* motivate of the leaders who will be commanding you to kill … for 'the cause,' as opposed to the

propaganda those leaders put out? Are you certain that the ultimate motivate isn't financial or political gain .for certain people in high places? ... Given what we know about the corrupting influence of demonic powers in all nations, and given what we know about how the American government ... has at times misled the public about what was really going on in the past (*e.g.*, the Vietnam War), these questions must be wrestled with seriously.

Moreover, even if a government is not lying to its people, "commanders often make poor decisions about particular battles they engage in that are not just and that gratuitously waste innocent lives" (p. 172).

B. Rebuttal

Boyd is correct on many of these points. As a result of man's fall and sin permeating every human institution, governments or individual politicians may lie or mislead their people (consider Watergate, the Iran Contra Affair, breached promises relating to Vietnam and the Lewinski Scandal). This does not however minimize the need for Christians to engage in their governments or their militaries. Rather, it *increases* the need for Christians that have been thoroughly been transformed by the Gospel of love and the love of justice, law and order to infiltrate governments and militaries to ensure that power is only used for good and just purposes and who will be accountable to their people and serve them with honesty and integrity.

It is also true, as Boyd points out, that commanders may make poor decisions about battles. Again, this increases the need for Christians who are committed to the Romans 13 God-ordained institution of government as the guardian of law and justice to join militaries as commanders who will be committed to excellence, doing all things "with all your heart, as to the Lord and not to men" (Col 3:23), who will abide by the Geneva Conventions on the protection of persons in armed conflicts while also looking to the safety of their teams and who will only assign their divisions to operations having reasonable chances of success.

VII. CHRISTIANS SHOULD NOT DEFEND THEIR RIGHTS

A. Boyd's Argument

Boyd cites a critique to his argument that states that if Christians do not stand up for their rights, their rights will eventually become extinguished: "Christians have a responsibility to take a strong public stand now to stop this slippery slope into a culture that may eventually make being a Christian illegal" (p. 178-79). To this, Boyd asks: "When id Jesus ever concern himself with protecting his rights or the rights of the community he was founding? Did he not rather do the exact opposite and teach us to do the same? He had all the power in the universe at his disposal and had every right to use it, yet out of love he let himself be crucified" (p. 181). Boyd does not fear the right to be a Christian or to be ablet o witness into people's lives.

B. Rebuttal

It is easy for Boyd to make these arguments from the refuge of America with all of her religious freedoms. Founded on Christian principles of tolerance and religious freedom, it would be easy or Boyd to argue that these rights are not so important, because he never experienced the hardship of Christians living in an Islamic country that severely restricts the rights of non-Muslims or that execute Muslims that convert to Christianity or in a communist country that forbids the possession of Bibles or forbids the practice of Christianity.

From the perspective of a Christian with all of the privilege of being an American citizen and the luxury of religious freedom, it is easy for Boyd to belittle the important freedoms that Christians have in America. But would he be so optimistic if he lived in an Islamic theocracy where he would not even be permitted to publish his books on Christianity? Would he be eager to give up his rights in a communist country where he was not even permitted to possess the Bible?

Living in a country that violate religious liberty and that makes the job of Christians to go into the world and preach the Gospel to all nations (Mar 16:15) would likely change Boyd's view on religious liberty. The critical task of working towards the salvation of souls is facilitated in a land where one may speak freely of his religion. In other countries that ban proselytization and books and web sites that preach the Gospel, reaching locals with the Gospel is that much more difficult. Because Christians recognize that there will be freedom where the spirit of God is (2Co 3:17), and that God seeks dominion over every area of our lives, they will work to protect the rights of people to read and possess the Bible, profess the Christian faith and spread it to all nations.

VIII.   GENERAL REBUTTAL

A. The Gospel Gives Legitimacy to Militaries

1. John the Baptist

As St. Augustine observed, if Christianity "forbade war altogether, those who sought salutary advice in the Gospel would rather have been counseled to cast aside their arms, and to give up soldiering altogether. On the contrary, they were told: 'Do violence to no man ... and be content with your pay'" (Thomas Aquinas, *Summa Theologica*, II-II, q. 40 a.1 (quoting Augustine)). If John the Baptist commanded soldiers to not intimidate anyone or accuse falsely, and be content with their pay (Luke 3:14), then he was at least implicitly giving legitimacy to militaries.

John the Baptist was a forerunner of Jesus, preaching that "kingdom of heaven is at hand" (Mat 3:2). His message was a prophecy of the kingdom of heaven to come. If John the Baptist commanded soldiers to be content with their pay, we can conclude that the kingdom of heaven that Jesus brought does not forbid soldiering.

2. Jesus Praises the Centurion

a. Jesus Does Not Hesitate to Point Out Sin

Jesus makes some harsh condemnations in Scripture. He condemned the scribes and Pharisees as "hypocrites" who are like "whitewashed tombs which indeed appear beautiful outwardly, but inside are full of dead men's bones and all uncleanness" (Mat

23:27). He drove out those who bought and sold at the temple and "overturned the tables of the money changers and the seats of those who sold doves" (Mat 21:12), making "a whip of cords" and driving them "all out of the temple, with the sheep and the oxen" (Joh 2:15).

Where sin needed to be corrected, Jesus did not hesitate to point it out. He told the woman who was caught in adultery to "go and sin no more" (Joh 8:11). When the Samarian asked Jesus to give him the water so that she would no longer thirst (Joh 4:15), Jesus asked her to call her husband (Joh 4:16). Indeed, Jesus was pointing out an area in the woman's life that was not right with God: she had five husbands and the one she was with at that time was not her husband (Joh 4:18).

b. Yet Jesus Does Not Point Out the Sins of the Centurion; Rather, He Praises Him

When Jesus entered Capernaum, a centurion pleaded with Jesus to heal his servant. He said that he was not worthy of Jesus' coming under his roof, but only asked that Jesus "speak a word, and my servant will be healed" (Mat 8:5-8). Jesus marveled at his faith, and declared that he had "not found such great faith, not even in Israel" (Mat 8:10). After he praised the centurion, He did not command him to give up his arms or resign from the military. Rather, he tells him, "Go your way; and as you have believed, so let it be done for you" (Mat 8:13).

3. God Was Pleased with the Centurion Cornelius; A Second "Devout Soldier (Acts 10)

Besides the example of the centurion whose faith is praised by Jesus, discussed above, we can look to the centurion Cornelius for another example of a soldier who was praised by God. He is highly regarded as a "devout man and one who feared God with all his household, who gave alms generously to the people, and prayed to God always" (Acts 10:2), so much so that an angel of God came to him and declared that his prayers and alms "have come up for a memorial before God" (Acts 10:3-4). Cornelius is not only described as "a just man, one who fears God and has a good reputation among all the nation of the Jews," but also as one who was "divinely instructed by a holy angel" (Acts 10:22), and who was used to bring the Gospel of Christ to the Gentiles (Acts 10:35-48).

Moreover, Cornelius himself calls on a "devout soldier" (Acts 10:7). As these examples make clear, it is possible to be both in the military and a follower of God.

B. God Uses War to Punish Evil

Moreover, God uses war throughout the Old Testament to punish sin. For example:

1. Destruction as Punishment for Blocking the People of God from Realizing God's Will: Heshbon (Deu 2)

The Israelites "put to death everyone in the cities, men, women, and dependents" and "left no survivor."[1] This was a punishment to the people of Heshbon because their king Sihon would not let the Israelites pass through to inherit their land.[2]

2. Destruction as Punishment for Attacking the Israelites

a. Bashan (Deu 3)

God's destruction of Bashan was as punishment for Bashan's attacking of the people of Israel:[3] "So the LORD our God also delivered into our hands Og king of Bashan, with all his people, and we attacked him until he had no survivors remaining ... utterly destroying the men, women, and children of every city."[4]

b. Amalek (1Sa 15)

The prophet Samuel gave Saul these instructions from the Lord: "The LORD sent me to anoint you king over His people, over Israel. Now therefore, heed the voice of the words of the LORD. Thus says the LORD of hosts: 'I will punish Amalek for

---

[1] Deu 2:31-34.
[2] Deu 2:30.
[3] Deu 3:1-2.
[4] Deu 3:3-6.

what he did to Israel, how he ambushed him on the way when he came up from Egypt. Now go and attack Amalek, and utterly destroy all that they have, and do not spare them. But kill both man and woman, infant and nursing child, ox and sheep, camel and donkey.'" (1Sa 15:1-3). This was as a punishment to Amalek for having assisted Eglon king of Moab against Israel (Jdg 3:12-13).

3. Commanding the Israelites to Attack, Harass, and Ultimately Destroy as a Punishment for Harassing and Seducing the Israelites: the Midianites (Num 25)

After the Midianite women seduced the Israeli men at Peor, God commanded Moses to "Harass the Midianites, and attack them; for they harassed you with their schemes by which they seduced you in the matter of Peor and in the matter of Cozbi, the daughter of a leader of Midian, their sister, who was killed in the day of the plague because of Peor" (Num 25:17-18). The seduction of the Israelis led to a plague, and God sought to end the plague.

It is also important to note that Numbers 22:4-8 describes the complicity and co-conspiracy of the Midianites in joining the elders of Moab in trying to engage the services of the sorcerer Balaam in obtaining a curse against the Israelites. Though the Bible does not say so directly, the punishment levied against the Midianites in Num 25:17-18 may have also been due to these acts, which God ultimately thwarted by instead using Balaam to bless Israel.

God later commands Moses to "Take vengeance on the Midianites for the children of Israel. Afterward you shall be gathered to your people" (Num 31:2). Moses spoke to the people, telling them to "go against the Midianites to take vengeance for the LORD on Midian" (Num 31:3). The Israelites "killed the kings of Midian with the rest of those who were killed ... Balaam the son of Beor they also killed with the sword" (Num 31:8).

The Bible is not clear what this vengeance was for, but it is presumably the same that led God to command Moses to "Harass the Midianites, and attack them" in Numbers 25: the Midianites' seduction of the Israeli men. Moses tells the officers of the army: "Look, these women caused the children of Israel, through the counsel of Balaam, to trespass against the LORD in the incident of

Peor, and there was a plague among the congregation of the
LORD" (Num 31:16).

4. Destruction to Prevent the Israelites from Engaging in the
   Idolatry of Their Foes (Deu 7)

In Deuteronomy 7, God instructs the Israelites to "conquer and
utterly destroy" seven nations greater than Israel: "the Hittites and
the Girgashites and the Amorites and the Canaanites and the
Perizzites and the Hivites and the Jebusites."[5] This harsh treatment
is commanded to the Israelites in order to prevent them from
breaking the very first and most important commandment of God:
"You shall have no other gods before Me."[6] For this reason, God
later commands the Israelites to "destroy their altars, and break
down their sacred pillars, and cut down their wooden images, and
burn their carved images with fire."[7] Deuteronomy later makes
clear why God instructed the Israelites to destroy these nations: to
prevent the nations from teaching the Israelites "to do according to
all their abominations which they have done for their gods, and
you sin against the LORD your God."[8]

C. Not All Who Are in the Military Are Called to Violence; They May Also Heal, Advise, Deter Violence, Punish Wrongdoers, Etc.

Yet Boyd neglects the fact that not all that enlist in the military
are called to violence. There are doctors, nurses, engineers,
architects, lawyers, drivers and cooks in militaries. In the
American Army, there are even officers assigned with the task of
prosecuting soldiers who violated some aspect of the Uniform
Code of Military Justice or other laws.

It is theoretically true that any member of a military—enlisted
or commissioned, institutional or operational—may be called to
violence against other human beings. Yet the reality is that many

---

[5] Deu 7:1.
[6] Exo 20:3.
[7] Deu 7:5.
[8] Deu 20:18.

institutional members of militaries are in reality in the business of saving lives. Legal counsels are often called to advise commanders as to how to undertake military operations in a manner that is least destructive to human life and civilian objects. Military doctors and nurses are often called to save lives, not only lives of their fellow soldiers, but those of civilians or prisoners of war. Military commanders, if infused with a true love for peace and justice, will find ways to achieve state objectives with minimal harm to human life (e.g., establishing a no-fly zone or humanitarian corridors rather than sending ground troops into what may be a potentially bloody battlefield). In fact, any military, if exercising its power responsibly, will always resort to violence as a very last resort when a state objective can be obtained through other means.

D. Building Up Militaries May Be a Form of Building Peace because it Deters Potential Attackers

Moreover, Boyd's view that Christians cannot serve in the military overlooked the fact that most of what militaries are called to do (or at least can do) is deter violence by building up formidable defense mechanisms. For example, a nation with a powerful coast guard, missile shield and invasion detection capabilities can institute peace without ever having to send a soldier into battle. Enemies will refrain from attack due to the deterrent effect that a strong and capable military has. On the contrary, a nation that refuses to raise a military and insists on a purely pacifistic foreign policy may actually be inviting violence, for such a country may attract conquest and invasion. By refusing to defend the innocent against violence and murder, the net effect may be an increase in the measure of evil in the world.

CHAPTER 3. CHRISTIANS SHOULD PURSUE THE "KINGDOM UNDER" MODEL, NOT THE "SWORD" OF CIVIL GOVERNMENT

I. THE CIVIL AUTHORITY IS THE SERVANT OF GOD TO EXECUTE JUSTICE

Pastor Boyd frequently comes back to Romans, chapter 13 (*see, e.g.*, p. 19):

> For rulers are not a terror to good conduct, but to bad. Would you have no fear of the one who is in authority? Then do what is good, and you will receive his approval, for he is God's servant for your good. But if you do wrong, be afraid, for he does not bear the sword in vain. For he is the servant of God, an avenger who carries out God's wrath on the wrongdoer (Rom 13:3-4).

It is therefore very clear that the civil authority, through its various instrumentalities (courts, executive body, police, prisons and, presumably, military), is an instrument used to carry out God's justice.

It should thus be clear that if a civil authority is unjust—arbitrarily meting out justice and persecuting minorities and political opponents rather than prosecuting true criminals, then it has failed to be an instrument of God's justice. In this sense, one can judge a civil authority through the lens of Scripture according to the extent to which it fulfills its God-ordained purpose of serving as "God's servant for your good" (Rom 13:3-4). Therefore, through the lens of Scripture, a government can be said to be "good" or "legitimate" if it is just and secures peace, law and order and "illegitimate" if it is the source of violence, injustice and disorder.

This is made clearer by 1Ti 2:1-2, which exhorts that "supplications, prayers, intercessions, and giving of thanks be made for ... for kings and all who are in authority, so that we may lead a quiet and peaceable life in all godliness and reverence." The idea expressed here is that by praying for our rulers, we may be able to lead a quiet and peaceable life. In other words, the civil authorities, when fulfilling their proper goal, are instruments that enable us to live peaceful lives and cultivate godliness and reverence in our lives.

There is therefore a scriptural basis for judging governments as good or bad. This can be contrasted with Pastor Boyd's moral vacuum, where all human government is equally depraved and irrelevant to God's greater Kingdom purposes.

II. WE ARE THEREFORE TO "HONOR THE EMPEROR"

Pastor Boyd goes on to remark that because of government's good function, Christians are to "honor the emperor" (1Pe 2:17) (p. 20). He cites Rom 13:1 ("Let every person be subject to the governing authorities. For there is no authority except from God, and those that exist have been instituted by God") and Tit 3:1 ("Remind them to be submissive to rulers and authorities, to be obedient, to be ready for every good work"), unless, of course, the laws of the land "conflict with our calling as citizens of the kingdom of God" (p. 20), for "We must obey God rather than men" (Acts 5:29).

We should also pray for civil leaders. Paul writes that his desire is that we pray for kings and all those in authority, so that we may have a calm and quiet life in all fear of God (1Ti 2:1-2).

III. YET THE WORLD IS IN UNDER THE POWER OF SATAN

The mere fact that civil government is instituted by God does not on its own mean that governments are righteous. As Pastor Boyd recognizes, "the whole world lies under the power of the evil one" (1Jo 5:19) (p. 21). "[F]allen principalities and powers (Eph. 2:2; 6:12) strongly influence our government, and every government, however relatively good that government may otherwise be" (p. 22). Civil government is thus instituted as a servant of God. Yet it is under the control of Satan.

IV. CHRISTIANS SHOULD THEREFORE SEEK CHRIST'S "POWER-UNDER" KINGDOM AND SHUN THE "POWER-OVER" KINGDOM

Believers should therefore "strive to be good citizens, praying and working for peace and justice [and] always practice a healthy suspicion toward the 'power over,' sword-wielding government they are subject to" (p. 22).

Boyd states that (p. 57):

> Until the kingdom of God transforms the entire globe, conflict is inevitable. This is not in any way to suggest that kingdom-of-God people should not pray nad strive for peace in the world, for we are called to be peacemakers (Matt. 5:9). Though we are not 'of' the world, we *are* 'in' it".

Here Boyd implies that Christians should be involved in the physical world. But "the only way to move toward this goal is for kingdom-of-God citizens to exercise 'power under' rather than 'power over'" (p. 57). So it would seem that Boyd is opposed to Christians' participating in the "power over" structures of the kingdom of the world—including militaries, police forces, legislative bodies and courts of law. These instrumentalities are ultimately flawed and in any case, heavily influenced by demonic forces. He concludes chapter 3 ("Keeping the Kingdom Holy") with (p. 66):

> We need not be able to figure out how society should tax its citizens, enforce inheritance laws, or deal with prostitutes. Neither Jesus, nor Paul, nor any New Testament author gave inspired pronouncements about such matters. But that does not prevent us from washing the feet of overly taxes citizens, disgruntled younger brothers, and despised prostitutes.

That Christians should not concern themselves with the issues that are handled through "power-over" structures is made clear on the back cover of the book: "Jesus taught us to seek a 'power-under' kingdom, where greatness is measures by sacrifice and service ... Dr. Boyd challenges readers to return to the true love of alvary and the message of the cross—setting the 'power over' politics of worldly government aside" (back cover).

Boyd writes that "only when everything in heaven and on earth has been purged by the fire of Gods's loving judgment (2 Peter 3:7, 10, 12) will the fundamental problems of the world be eradicated. And the only way to move toward this goal is for kingdom-of-God citizens to exercise 'power under' rather than 'power over.' It happens only as the mustard seed of the kingdom of God (cf. Matt. 13:31-32) grows through individual and corporate replications of Calvary" (p. 57). Again, Boyd leaves no room for Christians redeeming the "power over" of the civil authorities or participating in their justice. We are to focus only on Calvary-like love.

Boyd highlights the power and effectiveness of prayer, a "power under" resource, as contrasted with the "power over" of violence and military conquest. He reminds the reader of just how powerful prayer can be. Had there been but one intercessor for Jerusalem, the destruction of that city would have been averted (Eze 22:29-31). The land would have been spared, but God found not a single intercessor (p. 117-18). Boyd challenges the reader: "Dare we accept that it's not primarily the righteousness or sinfulness of a nation that determines whether God blesses or curses it, but the presence or absence of prayer on the part of those who call themselves his people?" (p. 118).

V. JESUS DID NOT GIVE IN TO THE TEMPTATION TO DO GOOD BY PARTICIPATING IN THE KINGDOM OF THE WORLD'S POWER STRUCTURES, SO NEITHER SHOULD WE

In speaking of Satan's temptation of Jesus in the wilderness (Luke 4:6-8), Boyd writes that "[w]ithout having to suffer and die, Jesus could have immediately taken a position as the functional lord of all [of the world's] kingdoms. True, Satan would have remained over him. His rule, therefore, would have had to participate in the 'system of domination' that runs the world. But at the very least, Jesus' position of power would have made the world a whole lot better. He could have quickly overpowered evil in all societies ... and created a kingdom of the world that enacted perfect law, order, and justice ... Yet Jesus refused. Why? Because

Jesus didn't come to make the kingdom-of-the-world a new and improved version of itself, let alone a Christian version of itself. Instead, he came to transform the 'the kingdom of the world' into 'the kingdom of our Lord and of his Messiah … He came to ultimately put the kingdom of the world out of business by establishing a counter-kingdom of radical love that would eventually render it obsolete" (p. 73-74).

This kingdom-of-the-world assumption—to conquer the world for the glory of God—is in essence the very thing the Devil tempted Jesus with. What makes the assumption so tempting is that it makes so much sense. How could society fail to be better off if we who know the truth are empowered to get our way in society?" (p. 96).

VI. GENERAL REBUTTAL

A. Just because Jesus Did Not Do Something Does Not Mean Christians Should Not Do It

Boyd asks the reader to consider these questions: "Did Jesus ever suggest by word or by example that we should aspire to acquire, let alone take over, the power of Caesar? Did Jesus spend any time and energy trying to improve, let alone dominate, the reigning government of his day? Did he ever work to pass laws against the sinners he hung out with and ministered to? Did he worry at all about ensuring that this right and the religious rights of his followers were protected?" (p. 92). The answer to these questions is, of course, a resounding "no."

Boyd later reminds the reader that "Jesus didn't concern himself with fixing or steering the Roman government. He entrusted this matter to his Father and allowed himself to be crucified by the Roman government" (p. 175). The implication is that Christians too should not be concerned with fixing their governments; they should instead direct all of their attention to living out radical Christ-like love.

Yet it would be wrong to conclude that because Jesus did not participate in the kingdom of the world, Christians should also not participate. Jesus did not do many things: he did not write

Christian music or poetry, create Christian paintings or other artwork, produce films that glorify God or found an organization that would protect vulnerable women and children from trafficking. Yet just because Jesus did not do these things does not mean that Christians should not do them.

What is important is that Christians infiltrate every aspect of society and shine as lights for Christ. Everything they do must be done in a spirit of love—whether it is starting a charity, founding an orphanage or running for political office. When we follow Christ's spirit of love and do all things for others, coming other them in love and service, our occupation may take a variety of different forms.

We must also remember here that Jesus had a unique mission. He was called to establish the kingdom of heaven. While Christians are called to build this kingdom, they are not called to found it. Nor are they forbidden from participating in the kingdom of the world, contributing towards its improvement, no matter how flawed or imperfect it may be.

B. Seek the "Power-Under" Kingdom, Redeem the "Power-Over" Kingdom

As Christians, we can ignore the reality of the demonic forces in the world and focus our complete attention on the spiritual realm, preparing ourselves for the kingdom of heaven and spreading the Gospel. Or we can focus on the spiritual realm while also acting towards the redemption of the physical world, what Pastor Boyd calls the "kingdom of the world" (or "kingdom of the sword"), thus joining in the redemption of the world by struggling towards good governance, justice, law and order.

1. Shunning Boyd's Strict Dichotomy

Boyd recognizes that "as American citizens, we can use our access to government to make the kingdom of the world as just as possible" (p. 125). But for him, the discussion ends there. He does not elaborate on how this is possible or what channels the Christian may pursue because the kingdom of the world provides "limited options" (p. 125). However, "as kingdom-of-God citizens, we need not, and must not, wait for these issues to be resolved before we act. Our trust, time, energy, and resources must not be centered on improving government but on living out the revolutionary kingdom of Jesus Christ" (p. 125).

I find no need for the strict dichotomy that Boyd lays out. As we are in the world, we are all citizens of kingdoms of the world. But as we are not of this world, we are simultaneously citizens of the kingdom of God. We should not eschew either one of them for the other. For we can be active citizens of God's kingdom by coming under people in love, while simultaneously striving towards the redemption of the physical kingdoms of the world by passing laws that institute order and justice, serving as judges administering law, joining police forces to "punish evil doers," for has has instituted these civil authorities to carry out his ultimate justice. Nothing in being a kingdom of the world citizen rules out being a kingdom of heaven citizen, unless one becomes intoxicated with the power or other idols that the kingdom of the world offers.

2. God Instituted Civil Government; Christians Are to Redeem It: the Creation-Fall-Redemption Metanarrative Involves Government

The fact that Scripture commands us to "honor the emperor" (1Pe 2:17) is a testament that the civil authority has not lost all of its God-given mandate. It has not fallen into so much depravity that man is to resist it fully, as would be the case, for example, of a government that required us to disobey God (*see* Act 5:29).

Therefore, we must recognize that civil government is in a struggle: it is under Satan's control, but no more so than death, disease, hunger, war and sin. Christians are not to give up these things as inherent to the kingdom of the world. Rather, we are called to spiritual warfare against them. We are called to be peacemakers, to heal the sick, raise the dead. We are called to be like Jesus, who multiplied the bread. As Christians, we have a calling to infiltrate *every* part of creation, and bring to it the redemption of the cross. This includes governments—courts, congresses, police forces and militaries. We are to become leaders and ensure that governments fulfill their God-given mandate of instituting justice and punishing wrongdoers. We must abolish those forms of government that punish the innocent and reap disorder and disarray. We are to become leaders in militaries and ensure that every military operation is undertaken with the least amount of harm to life and civilian objects, and ensure that our militaries remain primarily forces of deterrence and are only employed as a last resort, when all diplomatic channels are exhausted, and employing our militaries for good, to save live and in humanitarian disasters, as when the US Navy provided relief to Haiti after the 2010 earthquake.

C. Christian Service in Government is not Incompatible with Participating in the Kingdom of the World

As Boyd argues so convincingly, the purpose of life is to love God and love, serve and look after the interests of others.

Living in Calvary-like love can take many forms. It can be in serving the poor, healing the sick and visiting prisoners. It can also mean freeing the oppressed, through kingdom of the world instrumentalities, such as laws, through, for example, enacting just laws or serving to execute them or working through public defense offices to defend the innocent or bring justice to the guilty. One need not completely shun the kingdom of the world institutions which God has ordained when living Calvary-like love.

Yet we must remark that nothing about carrying out this purpose is incompatible with participating in government to fulfill God's justice mandate. It appears that Boyd would not disagree with this, for he writes that Christians, "along with all decent citizens, should work against unjust laws by political means, [but] our distinctive calling *as kingdom people* is to go far beyond this and manifest Calvary-quality love" (p. 184). Therefore, one should not conclude that participating in the Romans 13 civil institutions is in any way incompatible with being a loving, committed Christian.

D. Should We Give Into the Temptation?

We are all called to advance the kingdom of Calvary-like love. But we are not all called to be full-time pastors. Many of us are called to be workers in the kingdom of the world—social workers, manufacturers, architects, entrepreneurs, teachers, and even politicians, military officers, diplomats, lawyers and judges. These latter groups hold posts within the powers of the kingdom of the world. This is not contrary to their Christian calling. Just as they can serve their neighbor in Calvary-like love, so too can they work towards building social institutions that build towards justice, law and order, helping carrying out God's Romans 13 will for the civil authority. Just because the powers of this world are subject to the powers of Satan does not mean that Christians should not put on their armor of God (Eph 6:11) and infiltrate government. Our bodies are also subject to Satan, and he has inflicted death and sickness on it, but this does not mean that we are not called to oppose Satan and heal the sick and raise the dead, as did Jesus, Elijah and the disciples.

E. The Gospel Gives Legitimacy to Civil Service

The Apostle Paul concludes the book of Philippians saying, "All the saints greet you, but especially those who are of Caesar's household" (Php 4:22). There were therefore believers within the instrumentalities of civil government. If there were a divide so grave between the kingdom of God and the kingdom of the world that one could not be a citizen of both, then these "saints" would have quickly left Ceasar's household and dedicated themselves to ministry or some other calling outside of civil service.

F. Boyd Says the Answer is in Prayer; But Prayer Must Be Accompanied by Action

Pastor Boyd says the answer is in prayer. However, prayer must be accompanied by action. In fulfilling Christ's command to "make disciples of all the nations" (Mat 28:19), the twelve disciples did not just get on their knees and pray for conversions. While prayer was certainly a part of their ministry, they actively went out and preached the Gospel, and *were* the Gospel, healing the sick and preaching the Gospel. Peter commanded the lame man at the gate of the temple to rise up and walk in the name of Jesus, giving his feet and ankles strength (Acts 3:2-6). Paul "entered the synagogue and reasoned with the Jews" (Acts 18:19). Apollos spoke "boldly in the synagogue" (Acts 18:24-26) and "vigorously refuted the Jews publicly, showing from the Scriptures that Jesus is the Christ" (Acts 18:28). None of these disciples passively struggled against sickness or unbelief; they actively engaged the physical world around them.

Boyd argues that living in radical love means refraining from paying evil with evil. We are to leave judgment to God: "Paul says we are never to 'repay anyone evil for evil' and 'never avenge [ourselves].' All judgment is to be left to God (Rom. 12:17-19) who, among other things, uses governments to repay wrongdoers (Rom. 13:4)" (p. 40). If governments are used by God to effect His will, then is it inconceivable to conclude that God might call Christians to government? Since justice is part of God's will, it should not be doubted that God would call Christians to serve in government, participating in the system that God has ordained to repay evildoers and thus implement justice.

CHAPTER 4. AMERICA IS NOT AND NEVER WAS A CHRISTIAN NATION

I. ALL GOVERNMENTS ARE UNDER A COSMIC RULER OPPOSING GOD

Dr. Boyd concedes that "a particular political ideology may be better than others at preserving justice, law, and order," but "we must never forget that even the best political ideology lies under the influence of a 'power over' cosmic ruler who is working at cross-purposes to God" (p. 22).

II. SOME NATIONS MAY BE BETTER THAN OTHERS AT PRESERVING JUSTICE, BUT THIS DOES NOT MAKE THEM CHRISTIAN

"A nation may have noble ideals and be committed to just principles, but it's not for this reason Christian" (p. 54).

"To be sure, a version of the kingdom of the world that effectively carries out law, order, and justice is indeed closer to God's will for *the kingdom of the world* ... But no version of the kingdom of the world is closer to the kingdom of God than others because it does its job relatively well. For God's kingdom looks like Jesus, and no amount of sword-wielding, however just it may be, can ever get a person, government, nation, or world closer to that. The kingdom of God is not an ideal version of the kingdom of the world ... [It] is a completely distinct, alternative way of doing life" (p. 55).

III. AMERICA NEVER WAS FOR GOD: THE SLAUGHTER OF NATIVE AMERICANS, SLAVERY AND AMERICA'S OTHER SINS

Gregory Boyd is mystified by the phrase "Take America Back for God." He writes: "If we are to take America *back* for God, it must have once belong to God, but it's not at all clear when this golden Christian age was" (p. 98). He asks whether this "golden age" was when the American settlers (p. 98):

- 'Discovered' America and carried out the doctrine of 'manifest destiny'—the belief that God destined white Christians to conquer the Native Americans and steal their land, massacred Native Americans by the millions, broke almost every covenant they ever made with them, and then forced survivors into reservations; or
- Loaded *five to six million* Africans on ships to bring them to America, enslaved the roughly *three million* who survived the trip and acquired remarkable wealth through the slaves' labor.

As discussed below, Boyd's account of slavery in America and white-Indian relations is one-sided, oversimplified and ignores important nuances of the historic record.

IV. AMERICA STILL IS NOT A CHRISTIAN NATION: GREED AND IDOLATRY IN MODERN AMERICA

Not only is America's past marked by oppression and injustice, but America's present continues to be marked by sin. Greed, gluttony, divorce and idolatry are just a few of the sins that mark America.

"Despite what a majority of Americans say when asked by pollsters, we are arguably no less self-centered, unethical, or prone toward violence than most other cultures" (p. 113). America thus has her sins. Yet according to Boyd, the right is obsessed with demonizing homosexuals and banning abortion, despite the legion of other sins that the right neglects. This makes clear that although the Scriptures never grade sins, evangelical Christians do. "The fact that many evangelicals are publicly more upset about gay marriage than about divorce and remarriage, greed, gluttony, violence, and many other things is a case in point" (p. 139).

Dr. Boyd explains that it is America's greed, violence and sexual immorality, mixed in with hypocrisy in its desire to "spread freedom," that causes animosity towards America (p. 110):

> Not only does America represent greed, violence, and sexual immorality to them, but they view America as exploitive and opportunistic. To their way of thinking, for example, the 2002 invasion of Iraq, largely in defiance of the United Nations, on the later disproven grounds that Saddam Hussein posed an 'imminent threat' because he was building 'weapons of mass destruction,' simply confirms a long history of U.S. aggression under the guise of 'spreading freedom.'

V. GENERAL REBUTTAL

A. Is Christianity Irrelevant to the Question of Good Government? No; Democracy is the Way

The above statements are true. So we should not completely set aside the "power-over" politics of the world. If some political forms are better at preserving justice, law and order than others, then we as Christians should strive to implement these forms. And what is beautiful is that, of all of the forms of government available to men, it is democracy that is most compatible with Christian values. Just as Christians are to live for and serve others, so too are democracies set up, where political leaders are instituted by the people to serve them. Inasmuch as a political leader in a democracy puts personal gain over serving the common good, he is cast out of office through popular elections. A system of government where leaders are held accountable through free courts and a free press and are evaluated by the extent to which they come under and serve their constituents is the closest to the Christian ideals of self-sacrifice and value that any worldly government can come to. It reflects Christianity far more than any other form of government available today, including military dictatorships and tyrannical forms of governments that implement control by instituting fear and absolute dictators with no power checks in place.

B. Can a Government Look Like Calvary?

1. Overview

I would contend that a government that seeks to pillage and destroy its citizenry through the power of the sword cannot look like Calvary. However, a government that genuinely seeks to serve its people can.

A democratic country necessarily requires its officials to serve their people. If politicians in a democracy with a free press and free civil society come into office, give themselves salary increases and rob and pillage public treasuries (as is the case in many dictatorships around the world), word will come out and these officials will be fired at the next elections. If, in contrast, these officials true serve their people, in a self-sacrificial manner, their chances of rising up in the ranks and being given further responsibility will increase.

2. An Extreme Example

Suppose in country A, all of the leaders are democratically selected as the people as their servants, instituted to further the interests of the people. These representatives work diligently to provide for a system of law, order, justice and peace.

In country B, a military coup takes and keeps power through violence. It terrorizes its opposition by arresting, imprisoning and torturing those who oppose it. It is responsible for the kidnapping and death of thousands of people.

It would be difficult to find such a clear-cut, black and white example in reality, but we can at least concede that there are governments, such as Western democracies that *generally* respect human rights, which can be contrasted with states such as, for example, the former Soviet Union, which has been documented to have caused the death or disappearance of between three to sixty million civilians. Can we not contrast these two alternative systems of government and argue that western democracies come at least a little closer to realizing God's will for civil government than do countries that follow the Soviet Union's path?

3. Conclusion: Gregory Boyd Should not Be a Relativist with Respect to Government

Isn't a free democracy, one that allows you to freely worship God and to openly publish books as you have done in seeking to edify other believers a better government than one that prohibits your very right to criticize it? Isn't a democratic government that allows its citizens to freely explore life's purpose better than one that forbids reading or possessing the Bible or other religious material that can lead one to eternal life?

C. Is America as Bad as Boyd Says? Challenging Boyd's Oversimplified Account of American History

1. Treatment of the American Indians

Boyd's characterization of white-Indian relations is oversimplified, one-sided and fails to reference the role that law and voluntary transfer played in America's acquisition of Indian land. Valuable consideration was exchanged for the right to use or purchase territory from the Indians, including the island of Manhattan, which, according to a 1626 letter written by Dutch merchant Pieter Schage, was purchased for the value of 60 Dutch guilders.

As Stuart Banner writes in *How the Indians Lost Their Land: Law and Power on the Frontier* (Harvard University Press): "Much more land was obtained by purchase than by conquest" (p. 26). He points to numerous legal records of Indian property rights, including court cases that restored to American Indians land seized by whites and the "sheer number of surviving deeds by which Indians sold their land to English colonists," some of which "cover enormous areas" (p. 26). He quotes William Johnson, a colonial leader who observes that the "Indians had come to realize the value of their land, and indeed had 'grown so cunning and tenacious of their property that in short it is very difficult to get land from them without paying too much for it'" (p. 78).

Banner also discusses the practical benefit to purchase over conquest. The English preferred an orderly manner of legal transfer of title rather than conquest in order to avoid constant warfare with the Native Americans. Henry Knox, George Washington's Secretary of War, remarks that it would be "much less expensive for the United States to purchase" land from the Indian tribes than to wage constant war with them (p. 130-31).

This is not to suggest that all of the land transferred to the whites was completely voluntary. Despite treaties signed between the United States and the Indian nations following Andrew Johnson's Indian Removal Act, much of the westward migration of the Indians was through coercion (consider the Trail of Tears) or outright war (*e.g.*, the Second Seminole War of 1835-42). Nor is it to suggest that the United States performed all of its promises to the Native Americans (consider the 1832 Treaty with the Chickasaw, where the United States breached its promises to provide the Chickasaw nation with western land and protect them until they moved).

The question of white-Indian relations is more complicated than Boyd suggests. However, Stuart Banner's book and others in the field, including Richard White's *The Middle Ground* (Cambridge University Press) indicate the existence of serious scholarship portraying the Native Americans as active agents and negotiators of their own destiny. Yet Boyd ignores this scholarship and presents a one-sided account of whites as oppressors and Indians as victims, without any research to substantiate his claims.

2. Slavery in America

Dr. Boyd's account of slavery in America is also one-sided and unbalanced. He concludes that slavery as an institution is necessarily hostile to Christianity and that slavery as practiced by the American settlers is contrary to the Gospel, without ever justifying his conclusions.

a. Slavery as an Institution is Not Hostile to Christianity

Boyd begins by concluding that the institution of slavery is hostile to Christianity without any support to his conclusion. He fails to challenge the historic view that Christianity is neutral on the question of slavery or that Christianity condones slavery.

In reality, the Bible not only recognizes the institution of slavery, but also recognizes slaves as personal property (Exo 21:1 *et. seq.*). The Bible permits the Israelites to get slaves as property from among the surrounding nations (Lev 25:44). They may also purchase servants from among the children of aliens living among them and from their families born in their land, and these will be as property (Lev 25:45).

b. The Bible Seeks Not to Prohibit Slavery but to Infuse it with Justice

While the Bible does not prohibit slavery, it seeks to infuse slavery with justice and provide slaves with basic rights. For instance, if a master strikes his slave with a rod, causing death, he is to be punished (Exo 21:20). The slave was to rest on the Sabbath (Exo 20:10; Deu 5:14). The Israelites were not to be harsh masters over Hebrew slaves (Lev 25:46). An Israelite was not to return to his master a slave who has come to him in flight (Deu 23:15) or oppress him (Deu 23:16). When a master frees a fellow Hebrew slave, the master is to give freely to him in the measure of his wealth (Deu 15:14).

The Bible also seeks to protect the family unit within the institution of slavery. If a Hebrew slave was married when purchased, his wife is to go with him when he is freed in the seventh year (Exo 21:3). However, if his master gives him a wife, and he gets sons or daughters by her, the slave is to be freed by himself and the wife and her children are to remain behind as the master's property (Exo 21:4).

Furthermore, the Bible seeks to limit the duration of a slave's servitude. If an Israelite buys a Hebrew slave, he is to be a servant for six years, and in the seventh year he must let the slave go free without payment (Exo 21:2). However, this six-year limit only applied to Hebrew slaves. Slaves purchased from the children or families of aliens living in the land of the Israelites were to be kept as property for life and could be passed on to the children of the Israelites as an inheritance (Lev 25:46). Moreover, the six-year limit may be waived by a Hebrew slave: If he says does not wish to be free (Exo 21:5), then his master is to make a hole in his ear and he will be his servant forever (Exo 21:6).

c.   The New Testament Seeks to Infuse Slavery with Love

The New Testament affirms the institution of slavery. Although there is neither slave nor free (Gal 3:28; Col 3:11) in the sense that we are all one in Christ (Gal 3:28), Paul instructs slaves to obey their masters in all things (Col 3:24; Eph 6:5-7). What the New Testament seeks is to infuse slavery with Christian love. Paul therefore entreats slaves to obey their masters as servants of Christ, doing the pleasure of God from the heart (Eph 6:5-6). He instructs masters to do the same and prohibits them from using violent words or threats against slaves (Eph 6:9).

The idea of Christian love infusing all societal institutions, including slavery, is made most evident in Paul's letter to Philemon, a Christian in Colosse who was a slave owner. Paul writes on behalf of Philemon's former slave Onesimus, who after running away from Philemon, encountered Paul and converted to Christianity. Paul entreats Philemon to take back Onesimus "not as a slave, but as a brother" (Phm 1:16).

d.   History of Christianity on Slavery

It should therefore come as no surprise that the Church, given the absence of any scriptural prohibition, permitted the practice of slavery for over a millennium. Some church organizations, such as the Anglican Society for the Propagation of the Gospel in Foreign Parts, even owned slaves.

Many of the church fathers viewed slavery as the result of man's sin. St. Augustine wrote that the primary cause of slavery is sin: "[T]his is why we do not find the word 'slave' in any part of Scripture until righteous Noah branded the sin of his son with this name. It is a name, therefore, introduced by sin and not by nature" (St Augustine, *The City of God*, 19:15).

Thomas Aquinas in the thirteenth century went as far as attributing the institution of slavery to nature: "[M]en of outstanding intelligence naturally take command, while those who are less intelligent but of more robust physique, seem intended by nature to act as servants" (*Summa Contra Gentiles*). He does, in accordance with the Scripture, recognize the limits placed on masters and recommends that masters temper correction with mercy: "The command that masters should forbear from threatening their slaves may be understood in two ways. First that they should be slow to threaten, and this pertains to the moderation of correction; secondly, that they should not always carry out their threats, that is that they should sometimes by a merciful forgiveness temper the judgment whereby they threatened punishment" (*Summa Theologica*).

Only in the seventeenth century did some segments of Christianity, notably the Quakers and then Evangelical Christians, begin to question historic views of slavery as incompatible with biblical principles of equality.

e. Slavery as Practiced by the American Settlers is Contrary to the Gospel

Paul remarks of the love and faith that Philemon, a slave owner, has for Christ (Phm 1:5). And he never entreats Philemon to free his slaves! Rather, he entreats him to treat him fairly. This is the most powerful evidence that Paul condoned the institution of slavery. Paul entreats him to accept him *as a brother*. We see once again here that the Christian notion of slavery is not the institution—not the legal, social, contractual relationship between owner and slave—Christianity has no concern over this. Rather, it is love—the love that a slave owes to his master and his master owes to him. This shows that what is wrong with slavery is not the institution, but rather, abuse of slaves, which betrays Christian love.

One may therefore ask: since what the Bible prohibits is not slavery itself, but rather, abuse of slaves, was slavery as practiced by the American settlers contrary to the Bible? Dr. Boyd would answer with a resounding "yes," but the evidence points to a far more complicated answer. It is true that many slaves were abused by their masters in America. Boyd quotes Frederick Douglas as saying: "Between the Christianity of this land, and the Christianity of Christ, I recognize the widest possible difference—so wide, that to receive the one as good, pure, and holy, is of necessity to reject the other as bad, corrupt and wicked" (p. 101).

However, it must be conceded that the treatment of slaves varied widely in America. Some masters, in accordance with Christian charity, treated their slaves fairly and with mercy. As Harriet Beecher Stowe's classic *Uncle Tom's Cabin* demonstrates with poignant clarity, some masters conducted themselves in accordance with Christian principles of love and charity; others were abusive and subjected their slaves to degraded conditions and inhumane treatment.

One must recognize that the American Republic inherited the problem of slavery from Britain and was unable to abolish the practice immediately. The American founders confronted a degree of impracticality in freeing all slaves immediately upon independence. The founders recognized the degraded condition of black Americans, which posed a hurdle to granting blacks immediate citizenship. They also faced a majority of southerners that wishes to maintain slavery. The conundrum they faced was one that pinned universal equality and rights against the consent of the governed. The founders could not immediately emancipate slaves without betraying the consent of southern slaveholding states but it could not be true to the principles of freedom without emancipating the slaves.

The outcome we find in America was one of gradual emancipation. This is why northern states opposed counting slaves for the purpose of congressional representation. James Wilson, an anti-slavery northerner, proposed counting each slave as only three fifths of a free man in order to strengthen the antislavery majority in Congress. One finds a gradual prohibition of the slave trade and slavery in America, with all states north of Maryland having abolished slavery by 1804 (Dinesh D'Souza, *What's So Great About America*, p. 116). Many of the founders even went as far as planning to expatriate freed slaves back to Africa. By 1822, with the founding of Liberia as a colony for emancipated slaves, this vision became a reality.

While it is true that America needed to fight a destructive civil war in order to completely rid its territory of slavery, and that slavery as practiced in many parts of the south was brutal, abusive and oppressive, the one-sided account presented by Boyd and the conclusions he draws without any exploration as to contrary arguments, fails to recognize or engage the many nuances to the complicated history of slavery in America.

CHAPTER 5. GENERAL CRITIQUE: IS BOYD A RELATIVIST?

I. ENDLESS CYCLE OF EVIL

Dr. Boyd writes (p. 26):

> Fallen humans tend to identify their own group as righteous and any group that opposes them as evil. If *they* were not evil, we tend to believe, no conflict would exist. Hence, the only way to end the conflict is to 'rid the world of this evil,' as President George W. Bush said after the terrorist attach on the World Trade Center. The 'good' (our tribe) must extinguish the 'evil' (their tribe), using all means necessary, including violence.

One must question then whether Dr. Boyd believes *any* governmental action can be deemed good or evil. It seems he equates any act of State that involves violence as evil as any other act. Therefore, one state that implements force to exterminate a people is just as evil as another state that uses force to intervene and rescues that people. Each "tribe" believes its cause is justified and that the other "tribe" is evil. One must then question

II. DEMONIZING THE ENEMY TO CONVINCE CITIZENS TO SPILL BLOOD

"Every version of the kingdom of the world defends itself and advances its cause by rallying the self-interest of its citizens into a collective tribal force that makes each citizen willing to kill and be killed for what it believes to be the good of the society. It survives and advances by uniting and motivating its subjects around their distinct collective identity, ideals, self-interest, and desire for security—and against any individuals or governments whose own tribal identity, ideals, self-interest, and desire for security might impinge on or threaten their own. To this end, every version of the kingdom of the world demonizes its enemies when necessary to generate the motivation to go to war and to convince those who must spill blood that their cause is righteous" (p. 56).

Here, it seems that the possibility that some governments may actually have a just cause, or be qualified as "good" while others are qualified as "evil," is a remote and distant possibility to Dr. Boyd.

III. ARE THERE CORRECT ANSWERS TO POLITICAL QUESTIONS?

"Even if someone comes up with the 'correct' position on paying taxes (is there one?), what good does it do her if she loses her soul (Mark 8:30)?" (p. 61).

IV. BOTH SIDES IN A CONFLICT BELIEVE THEY ARE RIGHT

A. Boyd's Argument

Boyd argues that even if we concede that a Christian may participate in armed conflict if the cause is "just," a Christian would have great difficulty in determining whether a particular war is in fact "just" because "[f]ew wars have been fought in which both sides didn't believe their violence against the other side was justified. The reality is that the criteria one uses to determine what is and is not 'just' is largely a function of where one is born and how one is raised" (p. 170).

B. Rebuttal

A Christian need not allow cultural conditioning to inform whether a particular war is "just." There are objective criteria he can use in making such a determination.

1. The Natural Law

One may of course appeal to the natural law when determining whether a particular cause is just. "The work of the law written in the heart" (Rom 2:15). Therefore, man only needs to have a conscience unclouded by sin to clearly see right and wrong. This is why, for example, virtually all nations have ratified international treaties providing for the protection of persons in armed conflicts, limiting the weapons and methods of war and prohibiting genocide, crimes against humanity and war crimes. All 194 sovereign States have for example ratified the UN Charter, which severely restricts the use of force, and the 1949 Geneva Conventions, which protect civilians in armed conflicts. The fact that these treaties have such widespread acceptance demonstrates that there are certain principles that transcend the borders of nation-states and culture and that reflect a universal understanding of justice. On this basis, a citizen of a State that engages in genocide should in his heart know that his nation is engaged in evil and should therefore refrain from supporting State action. However, a citizen in a State that is fighting to stop genocide and reestablish should through the natural law understand that his State's war has a just cause and is waged with the right intention.

Of course, few scenarios in the reality of international politics are as clear cut as the above. Yet it would be wrong to conclude that such scenarios do not arise. For example, while it is true that both Franklin Roosevelt and Adolf Hitler believed that they were fighting a just cause, Adolf Hitler's view does not meet the rigors of natural law thinking, which condemns genocide. Germany's later apology for its acts under the Holocaust and former West German Chancellor Willy Brandt's 1970 falling on his knees in front of a Holocaust memorial in the Warsaw Ghetto, coupled with Germany's payment of billions to Israel and to Jewish survivors (see "The Holocaust " in "Top 10 National Apologies," *Time*, June 17, 2010), shows that even Germany recognized the evils of its wartime acts, albeit only retroactively.

2. International Law

a. *Overview*

International law provides another approach that the conscientious Christian can take in determining whether an act of aggression is "justified."

If it is determined that an act of aggression violates international law, then the conscientious Christian, is to abstain from in any way supporting it. Because the Bible establishes a system of civil government that establishes law, order and justice, a state or government that violates law ought to not be supported or defended. St. Paul instructs the believer to "put himself under the authority of the higher powers, because there is no power which is not of God, and all powers are ordered by God" (Rom 13:1). A president or emperor that contravenes his own international treaties and commitments under international law breaks his covenants and violates the biblical precept of order. Christians ought not to support his efforts.

b. Permitted Use of Force Under International Law

International law provides strict limitations on the use of force. Both customary international law as well as the UN Charter recognize the territorial integrity and independence of States and prohibit military force from interfering with this integrity. The Charter of the UN (CUN) states that "All Members shall settle their international disputes by peaceful means in such a manner that international peace and security, and justice, are not endangered" and that "All Members shall refrain in their international relations from the threat or use of force against the territorial integrity or political independence of any State, or in any other manner inconsistent with the Purposes of the United Nations" (art. 2 CUN).

Chapter VII of the UN Charter permits only two exceptions to these blanket prohibitions on the use of force. The use of force is permitted when acting pursuant to: (i) UN collective security measures (art. 42 CUN); or (ii) self-defense (art. 51 CUN).

The first exception is the right of the Security Council to employ the use of force in order to secure peace. If the Security Council determines the existence of any threat to or breach of the peace or act of aggression, it is to make recommendations or decide what measures are to be taken to maintain or restore peace (art. 39 CUN). In order to prevent an aggravation of the situation, the Security Council may "call upon the parties concerned to comply with such provisional measures as it deems necessary or desirable" (art. 40 CUN), and may decide what measures not involving the use of armed force (*e.g.*, sanctions, the severance of diplomatic relations, etc.) are to be employed to give effect to its decisions (art. 41 CUN). However, if these measures are inadequate or ineffective, the Security Council may as a last resort take military action (art. 42 CUN).

The second exception is the use of force pursuant to States' inherent right to self-defense. Defensive military acts may be taken by States as a last resort when threatened by armed attacks under article 51 of the UN Charter, which states that "nothing in the present Charter shall impair the inherent right of individual or collective self-defence." The right of States to act in self-defense is also embedded in customary international law. The CUN imposes certain requirements and restrictions on the right to act in self-defense. Acts undertaken in self-defensive are subject to immediate Security Council review. Furthermore, the Charter only permits the right to act in self-defense "*until* the Security Council has taken measures necessary to maintain international peace and security" (art. 51 CUN), that is, until the Security Council actually takes action.

3. Christian Just Law Theory

The third option that the Christian has in determining whether a particular armed conflict is appealing to Christian just law theory. Various denominations have elaborated the particular criteria of a "just" war. Perhaps among all of them, the Catholic Church has elaborated the most developed and precise theory.

The Catholic church has accepted just war theory on the basis that some rogue states cannot be led to accept peace, order and justice without resorting to the use of force. The Benedictine Monks of Solesmes, France, provide a succinct overview of the Catholic Church's teaching on the use of force in *Just War at the Service of the Divine Precept of Peace*, which observes that:

> [P]eace can have recourse to force. However, force, in itself, is
> incapable of restoring peace, since peace is the fruit of the union

of justice and charity. Some enemies of justice cannot be led to accept the necessary conditions for peace without the use of force. The importance of a certain good justifies entirely its defense by force against an unjust aggression (Moines de Solesmes, *La Paix Internationale*, Desclee, Paris, 1956, v. I, p. 20).

Saint Thomas Aquinas built upon the just war foundation developed originally by Augustine and introduced the concept of the common good as a necessary element in the legality of war. Aquinas then lays down his conditions for a war to be just. The war must be waged: (i) by a legitimate authority; (ii) with a just cause; and (iii) a right intention. The *Catechism of the Catholic Church* has expanded the three conditions set forth by Aquinas (legitimate authority, just cause and right intention) and further fleshed them out. Today, the Catholic Church requires a war to meet the following criteria in order for it to classify as "just":

- *Legitimate authority*. It must be waged by a legitimate civil authority (*i.e.*, a State, in accordance with Romans 13), not individuals or groups who do not constitute an authority sanctioned by whatever the society deems legitimate;
- *Just cause*. The cause must be just (*i.e.*, self-defense of the innocent against an armed attack, redressing an injury, punishing evil, restoring territory unjustly seized);
- *Right intention*. The central intention of the war must be re-establishing a just peace (not conquering, spreading seeds of revolt or acquiring power or material possessions);
- *Last resort*. All non-violent options must be exhausted before the use of force is justified;
- *Reasonable prospect of success*. Deaths and injury incurred in a war not having a reasonable chance of success are not morally justifiable.
- *Grave damage from the aggressor*. The damage inflicted by the aggressor on the nation must be lasting, grave, and certain;
- *Proportionality*. The use of arms must not produce evils graver than the evil to be eliminated; the peace established by the war must be preferable to the peace that would have prevailed had the war not been fought.

4. Conclusion

One will generally find that if a war is deemed just under the natural law, international law or Christian just law theory, it will also be deemed just under the other sets of criteria. This is because international law and Christian just law theory in many ways reflect natural law thinking and are based on conceptions of justice common to mankind across cultures. Moreover, the Christian just war theory of the Catholic Church parallels the conditions set forth under international law, as follows:

- *Legitimate authority*. Only the UN Security Council or a State acting in self-defense may legitimately wage war.
- *Just cause*. Only self-defense and quashing out threats or breaches to peace or acts of aggression are permitted.
- *Right intention*. The intention of collective security action is maintaining or restoring peace.
- *Last resort*. The UN Charter requires all non-violent methods of maintaining or restoring peace (calling upon "the parties concerned to comply with such provisional measures as it deems necessary or desirable" (art. 40 CUN); deciding what measures not involving the use of armed force (*e.g.*, sanctions, the severance of diplomatic relations, etc.) are to be employed to give effect to its decisions (art. 41 CUN)) to be exhausted before the use of force is permitted.
- *Proportionality*. This element is not found in international law regarding the legality of the use of war (*jus ad bellum*). However, it is carefully elaborated in international law governing conduct in war (*jus in bello*), which establishes two principles towards the protection of persons: (i) distinction (discrimination); and (ii) proportionality with respect to civilian losses. Distinction requires parties to a conflict to distinguish between the civilian population and combatants in order to spare civilian populations and property. Proportionality with respect to civilian losses requires those who plan military operations to take into consideration the extent of civilian destruction and probable casualties that will result and, to the extent

consistent with the necessities of the military situation, seek to avoid or minimize such casualties and destruction.

There are, however, two elements in the Catholic Church's just war theory that are not required criteria of the use of force under international law: (i) a reasonable prospect of success and (ii) grave damage from the aggressor resulting from an aggressor. However, while international law does not require an affirmative showing of either of these elements, they will certainly be considered as measures of prudence by the Security Council or by individual States acting in self-defense in the calculus as to whether to undertaken military action in a particular campaign.

CHAPTER 6. CONCLUSION

Dr. Boyd's book represents a departure from the biblical injunction to co-labor with God as redeemers in all aspects of creation. This of course means seeking justice for the needy, defending the fatherless, pleading for widows, visiting the distressed in their trouble, undoing heavy burdens, freeing the oppressed, feeding the hungry and healing the sick, in addition to proclaiming the Gospel to the ends of the earth. But our redemption calling does not stop there; it also means occupying every aspect of creation—whether in government, politics, the law, the military, law enforcement, media, academia, film, the visual arts and music, and reforming culture both by transforming individual lives and also transforming laws to reflect to a just civic order. In doing so, we will lay down the foundations of a world without tyranny—of free societies where all people may thrive, freely worship and serve God.

Made in the USA
San Bernardino, CA
10 July 2016